Selected Treasures

of

Greenfield Village

and

Henry Ford Museum

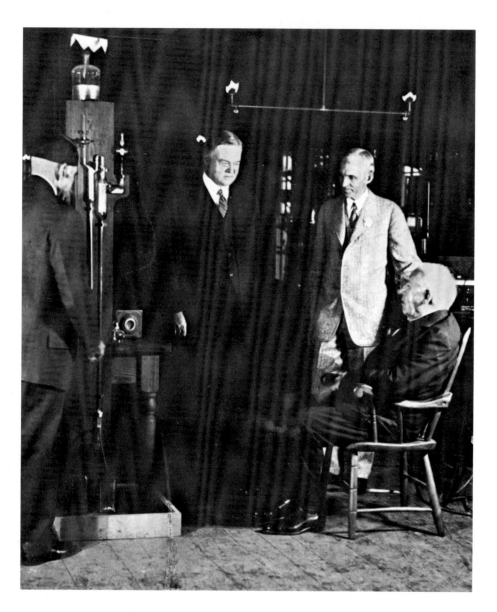

On the evening of October 21, 1929, in celebration of the 50th anniversary of Thomas A. Edison's creation of the incandescent lamp, over three hundred leaders, scientists, citizens and educators from all over the world gathered together at one of the most distinguished banquets ever held (see painting on pages 4-5 by Irving Bacon). Following the banquet, the aging inventor, President Hoover and Mr. Ford adjourned to the Menlo Park Laboratory, which had been newly re-erected in Greenfield Village. At that time Edison's re-creation of his first lamp not only signaled the anniversary of that immortal event, but it also symbolized the dedication of The Edison Institute in his honor.

Table of Contents

"I am collecting the history of our people as written into things their hands made and used," said Henry Ford of his great educational and historical project, *The Edison Institute,* at Dearborn, Michigan.

Here, in Greenfield Village, an *outdoor* museum, comprised of nearly 100 original buildings transported from all over the United States, and in the Henry Ford Museum, an *indoor* museum of American history, containing historic objects, books, manuscripts, and photographs covering virtually every phase of life in America, he planned to preserve, in three-dimensional form, the most important collection of American cultural and industrial *treasures* he could assemble for the enjoyment and edification of future generations.

He named them The Edison Institute in honor of the greatest genius (and friend) he had ever known, Thomas Alva Edison, whose mind, he felt assured, was one of the most creative the world had ever seen.

It is thus with great pride that our curators assembled the 40th Anniversary Exhibition entitled "Selected Treasures of Greenfield Village and Henry Ford Museum," only

a portion of which can be illustrated here. Drawn from every nook and corner of the Village and Museum, we hope it delineates in broad, incisive strokes the larger picture Mr. Ford sought both to illuminate and preserve: *the story of America's ideals and achievements under the free enterprise system.* "I deeply admire the men who founded this country," he said, "and I think we ought to know more about them and how they lived and the force and courage they had." And speaking of The Edison Institute on another occasion, "When we are through, we shall have reproduced American life as lived, and that, I think, is the best way of preserving at least a part of our history and tradition."

It was but a brief step from his collecting favorite *McGuffey Readers* in 1914 and restoring his own birthplace on its original site in 1919 (not far from where he would ultimately establish Greenfield Village), to his becoming Henry Ford, the indefatigable collector, sparked by his own restoration of Longfellow's Wayside Inn, 1923, Botsford Inn, 1924, and many other historic American shrines sadly in need of preservation in the early 1920's. Inevitably he became the first

Painting by Irving Bacon of the banquet held on October 21, 1929, celebrating the 50th anniversary of Edison's creation of the incandescent lamp.

Foreword

by

Dr. Donald A. Shelley

National Broadcasting Company microphone used during the banquet depicted above.

great pioneer to combine the collecting of Americana with the preservation of historic American buildings.

A labor of love and patriotism, no "treasure" was too remote, or too elusive, to escape his enthusiastic search, whether in this country or abroad. The museums and early settlements on the Eastern seaboard, as well as in Britain and on the Continent, became the yardstick as well as the source of his restless and relentless search. Enthusiastic letters of approval, newspaper accounts, even personal gifts of family treasures, poured in; cartoonists also "spoofed" his exaggerated efforts to select not just the best, but what in his view was the *most typical* American item.

In this exhibition, perhaps for the first time, we present an appraisal of the success of his efforts measured by modern standards. We are indicating in some measure the extent to which Mr. Ford's original plans for the development of The Edison Institute and its collections are being carried forward today: "to educate directly, and indirectly." We are also recording the progress and broadened activities of this great *general museum of American history established for educational purposes* where, each year, "American history comes to life" for nearly one-and-a-half million visitors of all ages. To date, nearly 30,000,000 persons from all over the world have passed through our doors.

Utilizing the matchless rural setting of Greenfield Village and the beautiful Decorative Art Galleries, Street of Shops, and Mechanical Arts Hall of the Henry Ford Museum (an architectural treasure in itself), our professional staff continues to implement and develop appreciation of our basic American ideals through educational activities involving this priceless collection. American history comes to life each day of the year through: 1, operating craft shops which perpetuate early home crafts or industries; 2, major special events or festivals actively involving Americana collectors groups or clubs; 3, the Museum's annual program of special exhibitions and demonstrations; 4, educational forums and seminars and; 5, more recently, our American Drama Festival which features original early American plays of historic nature presented by drama students.

The broad scope of the Americana collections assembled by Henry Ford is appropriately visible in the "treasures" selected by our curators for this 40th Anniversary Exhibition. Whether they stem from the picturesque and nostalgic "visual" covering 260 acres in Greenfield Village, or from his great three-dimensional study collection of full-size objects supported by almost limitless archives of printed, manuscript, and photographic background information, they have been studied carefully for possible inclusion in this exhibit. Not that everything could be fully analyzed and processed here, but rather that, if not included or illustrated, it might at least be present in the *checklists* of additional treasures at the close of each section. Where items were permanently installed, or too cumbersome to move to this exhibit, an illustration or listing is included herein.

Employing our Founder's philosophy that "a piece of machinery or anything that is made is like a book, if you can read it . . ." a number of guidelines for selecting treasures for the exhibit were agreed upon. Market value, or rarity alone, were only partial considerations involving the much broader perspective of American artistic, educational, social, industrial, and scientific history. It became obvious, after preliminary testing, that five or six different criteria would be required to assess fairly The Edison Institute's vast collection of Fine and Decorative Arts, Crafts, Tools and Home Industries, as well as its collections of Agriculture, Power, Lighting, Communication, and Transportation in all forms. In addition, invaluable primary resource materials from the Museum Research Library's books, manuscripts, and map and print collections, as well as from our unique Ford Archives holdings of original documents and photographs (received in 1964), likewise provided virtually unknown treasures.

Our Collections Staff came up with five excellent classifications which not only served for the Treasures Exhibit, but also for the divisions of this *Catalogue*:

1. Outstanding Historic Firsts
2. Historic Association Items
3. Masterpieces of Craftsmanship
4. Unique Examples
5. World's Largest Collections

These guidelines, it was felt, not only best represented the scope of the collections and are not mutually exclusive, but also reflect accurately Mr. Ford's philosophy and intent in bringing together, here at Dearborn, Michigan, on one property, such a varied and comprehensive assemblage of raw materials of American history.

It goes without saying, that numerous objects could easily, and logically, fit into two or three of these categories. Conversely, some items our Museum visitors may feel are of great importance might have been omitted altogether, but they would quickly acknowledge that even selection committees are only human. While gallery space available limited the current exhibition to slightly more than 100 of the several hundred items nominated, it is planned to deal further with the collections in greater depth in the near future. Meanwhile, as already mentioned, *checklists* of additional items are included at the end of each of the five divisions of this catalogue.

It is to be expected, no doubt, that the largest and most important single collection brought together here is Edisonia, since Edison himself assisted in gathering and completely furnishing some 8 or 10 original Edison buildings in Greenfield Village. He also collected for Mr. Ford's American history museum innumerable additional treasures covered by Edison patents.

The "Wizard of Menlo Park's" name in our collection would be followed by Washington, Webster, Foster, McGuffey, Lincoln, the Wright brothers, G. W. Carver, Burbank, Firestone, Heinz, Ford, and numerous others. By far the largest, most significant, most varied, individual gift received in recent years would be the Ford Archives in 1964, numbering some 14 million documents, books, manuscripts, and photographs; the latter collection preserves one of the richest pictorial records of all phases of the World War I period in existence.

As regards time and chronology, it can be said that our treasures actually stretch from European roots before the first settlers set sail for our shores in the 17th century, through the development of the American Colonies and their far-reaching struggle for Independence toward the end of the 18th century, through the political expansion and mechanical achievements of the 19th century with heavy concentration upon the effects of the Industrial Revolution upon America, and extend on down roughly to the beginning of World War II and the first signs of the Space Age.

Continual research and investigation, as well as up-dating and refining our collections over the past two decades, has served to strengthen them in every area of subject-matter. Collections temporarily "off exhibit" are being brought back, others present, but never shown, are being introduced, and totally *new dimensions* are being defined for other collections.

The strength of the collections, as well as the ability of The Edison Institute to implement their use (as with any live plant), is enhanced by constant cultivation and pruning. The Village and Museum thus continue to meet modern standards in today's world, to be an institution geared for people, to educate directly and indirectly, and to "bring American history to life" for ever larger numbers of citizens of America and the world.

The Edison Institute maintains one of the most active, cooperative programs in the country for Americana enthusiasts in every field of collecting related to our museum displays. It stimulates deeper appreciation and understanding of our American heritage, at the *grass roots* level, through encouraging collecting, preserving, and studying it in the home. The individual contributions of each State, of each nationality group, and of each social or religious background to the American way of life, are emphasized.

First electric lamp made at Dearborn on October 19, 1929, by Thomas A. Edison for Henry Ford, using a carbonized cotton sewing thread filament.

Outstanding Historic Firsts

The Firsts are the beginnings, the start of the evolutionary process that stretches across time to the very present. Through them, may be traced the steps which have led to the modern world.

In the Henry Ford Museum, starting with the replica of the "Rocket," the first practical steam locomotive built in England by George Stephenson in 1829, the movement turns to the DeWitt Clinton, the first locomotive in New York State and the third in America. Following are wood-burning locomotives of the Civil War period, and other 19th and 20th century American engines.

The Roper Steam Car, built in 1865 by Stephen P. Roper of Roxbury, Massachusetts, is the oldest existing American-built automobile. The 1903 Packard, "Old Pacific," was the first car to cross the United States entirely under its own power. The 1913 Ford Touring Car was the first model to be built on a moving assembly line, revolutionizing all manufacturing.

In the Wright Cycle Shop is housed much of the original machinery used by the Wright brothers in manufacturing the first airplane which led, in time, to the 1926 Fokker Tri-motor, the first airplane to fly over the North Pole, and to the 1928 Ford Tri-motor, the first to fly over the South Pole. The 1927 Boeing 40-B Airplane was the first to fly scheduled transcontinental passenger service in the United States. The 1939 Sikorsky Helicopter was the first practical helicopter produced in America.

The Newcomen atmospheric-pressure engine, invented by Thomas Newcomen in 1705 was the first commercially successful steam engine design. The engine shown, built *circa* 1750-60, was in use until 1830. Additional examples of progressively improved power development designs are on exhibit.

Thomas Alva Edison is represented in this area by his phonograph or talking machine; his mimeograph, the patent for which he sold to A. B. Dick of Chicago; his electro-harmonic telegraph of 1874; the platinum, cardboard and bamboo filament light bulbs of 1879 and 1880; his galvanometer of 1883; his kinetoscope of 1890; and his motion picture camera of 1890.

The first typewriter was completed about 1783 and Remington issued a factory-produced typewriter the following year. Stewart and Chickering built their first square piano at Boston, Massachusetts, in 1823. Singer produced his sewing machine in 1854. Armstrong developed a portable, self-contained battery-operated radio, *circa* 1922.

The "firsts" march on, from iron plows to wireless transmitters and audio tubes; from woodcut maps to manuscript materials and shares of stock.

Each of these "firsts" is a part of the American scene. Without it, at its particular place in time, we would be less than we now are.

Comparatively few photographs of Edison's early life exist; very few indeed are known to have been made. This original Daguerreotype, copies of which have been reproduced in a number of biographical accounts since the appearance of W.K.L. Dickson's work in 1894, is reputed to be the earliest known photograph of the lad "young Tom" who was to become one of the world's greatest inventors. It was taken in 1851 while the Edison family resided in Milan, Ohio. "Young Tom" or "Al" as his mother called him, was then four years old.

The laboratory built by Thomas Edison's father in 1876 was the first building to be erected in the Menlo Park Compound. In this unpretentious two-story clapboard structure Edison sought a quiet seclusion with his technical staff in a devoted effort to produce inventions which would be commercially practical. Among the four hundred or more inventions which Edison developed at Menlo Park are the phonograph, carbon transmitter, microphone, the electric railway, incandescent lamp and numerous other devices for which he is most famous. Although the most important contribution which Edison and his staff made at Menlo Park has been the development of a complete system of electrical engineering, it is often said that his greatest single invention was one which he never patented—namely, the development of organized technical research which he began practicing here in 1876.

The second floor was restored by Henry Ford, with Edison's personal assistance, to appear as it was during the invention of the first successful incandescent lamp. Fifty years to the day, Edison returned to the laboratory and re-enacted that incident in the presence of President Herbert Hoover, Henry Ford, and Francis Jehl.

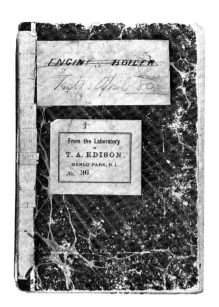

This small set, manufactured by the late Hugo Gernsback, one of the foremost pioneers in the history of commercial wireless promotion, was marketed in the form of a "do-it-yourself" kit in 1906. It was the first production wireless telegraph advertised for sale in the world. It utilized the electro-magnetic induction principle discovered by Edison in 1875, and later further defined by Hertz and Maxwell. This set operated by the transmission of wireless impulses by Morse Code.

The sewing machine made by the Singer Company in New York, *circa* 1854, shown right, is an excellent example of the earliest practical development of such a device beyond the crude model made by its inventor, Elias Howe. It has a reciprocity shuttle, vertical needle arm and wheel feed. It represents the first of a series of developments leading to the modern electric machines of today.

The Hanks Silk Mill, shown at far right, was originally located at Mansfield, Connecticut, and was built in 1810 by Rodney Hanks. It was the first power mill to produce silk in the United States. The mill was moved to Greenfield Village in 1931, where even today silk thread is produced directly from cocoons. A grove of Mulberry trees stands nearby; the leaves provide the necessary nourishment for the young silkworms.

This machine represents the first factory-produced typewriter patented by Christopher Latham Sholes and Carlos Glidden in 1868. Through joint consultation with Thomas A. Edison in 1871, a practical working keyboard was developed. Working on the "understrike" principle, this device printed in capital letters only. It was manufactured by the Remington Arms Company of Ilion, New York. United States patents embodied in this device were sold by Sholes and Glidden to Remington, creating one of the largest typewriter manufactories in the world.

This simple motion picture camera was made by Thomas A. Edison at West Orange, New Jersey in 1889. It was used in the first motion picture studio during the beginnings of the motion picture industry there in 1894. Originally the machine was driven by an electric motor, which was later removed and replaced by a hand propelled crank and set of gears. It is thought that this modification was made for demonstrational purposes during the patent suits with the Mutoscope Company in the late 1890's. This pioneer camera was given to The Edison Institute collection by Thomas A. Edison in 1929.

The first engine to operate on a four-stroke cycle and first to achieve compression of the charge within the working cylinder, was the so-called "smoke machine" invented by Nicolaus August Otto and Eugene Langen in 1866. It was covered under German patents issued to Langen, Otto, and Roosen, and is today recognized as the progenitor of all reciprocating engines operating on the internal combustion principle.

After the successful trial of the first phonograph in 1877, Edison entrusted Sigmund S. Bergmann with the task of manufacturing the first commercial lot of cylinder tin foil phonographs. He produced about six hundred of these devices. The machine used the foil as a recording surface. It was embossed with a pattern when a crank was manually turned and the mouthpiece spoken into. The voice was reproduced by rewinding the cylinder and allowing the needle to pass over the "recorded" surface.

This device, invented by Edison at Newark in 1875 and first manufactured at Menlo Park one year later, was designed to perforate innumerable holes in wax paper by the action of a needle being driven up and down in the end of a pen by a small electric motor. When this "stencil" was spanned in the frame of the hand press and an ink roller passed over its surface, ink would be forced through the perforations onto a clean sheet below, creating a duplicate of the original.

After several months of experimental research in an attempt to perfect a practical incandescent lamp, Thomas A. Edison applied for a United States patent on October 14, 1878. Allowed specifications and claims were granted to Edison on April 22, 1879, in the form of patent #214636 on an "improvement in electric lights." This, Edison's first lamp patent, made use of a thin platinum strip which was controlled electrically by the use of a thermostatic device. This "filament," as Edison later defined it, was brought to incandescence when a current was applied. When it achieved a temperature of a given degree, the circuit was broken by the thermostat thus lengthening the life of the lamp. The "filament" on this lamp did not burn in a vacuum.

The first commercial three-way wireless "Audion" valve or detector was invented by Dr. Lee DeForest, in 1907, and patented by him the following year. The significance of the DeForest invention over the Edison-Fleming vacuum tube was the addition of a third wire or grid placed between the filament and plate. This served as a controlling factor under the alternating negative-positive charges of incoming waves, thereby breaking the current flowing from the filament to the plate. This "Audion" action induced a replica of the incoming signals in the grid to headphone circuit, and served to somewhat amplify those impulses.

Although this "triode" principle was then little understood, it was utilized in the earliest "Audion" wireless receivers which were produced and marketed in 1908.

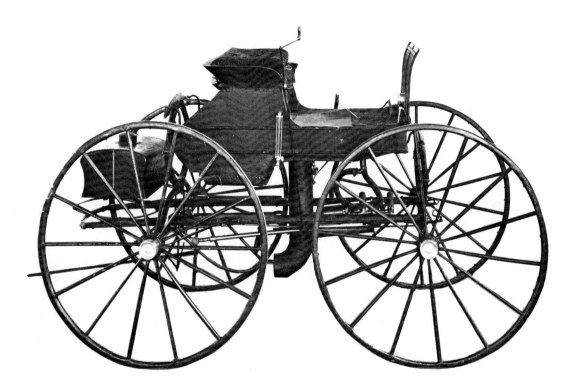

This Roper Steam Carriage, built in 1863 by Silvester Roper at Roxbury, Mass., is the oldest automobile in the United States. For two decades it was exhibited at county fairs in the north and midwest. Usually it was pitted against the best trotting horses and it always won. The Roper is driven by two oscillating cylinders with piston rods to the rear axle. Fuel for the underseat boiler was powdered coal or charcoal.

HERALD.

Pubished on the Mixed Train. June 1862

THE WEEKLY HERALD

PUBLISHED BY THE NEWSBOY ON THE MIXED TRAIN.

TERMS

Our Paper will be delivered to subscribers o the line of the Grand Trunk for eight cents per month in advance.

To Grand Trunk Agents—We would feel obliged to the several Agents along the line of the Grand Trunk Railway, if they would be kind enough to send their orders for the Hera'd to the Newsboy (T. Edison) Mixed Train Detroit Section. Inclose eight cents per month strictly in advance. N, B, Aall items gladly received.

ITEMS.

The Norfolk Navy Yard is not to be rebuilt.

The ship builders of Philadelpha never enjoyed more prosperous times than at present.

Gen Sickles left Washington on Tuesday to resume command of the Excelsior Brigade.

A vessel will sail from Baltimore for Liberia on the 15th of June by which emigrants can go.

In Toronto a crusade has been commenced by the authorities against the unlicenced grog-shops.

Col Corcoran is hourly expected at Norfolk under a flag of truce.

England.

Tom Sayers starts for Australia in September

The newspapers published in Great Britain number 1, 165,

John C, Heenen is showing in the south of Wales,

It is officially notified that Queen Victoria will this year hold no levee or drawing-room,

The celebrated English ratter Jacko recently finished 1558 rats in the marvellously quick time of 5min & 28 sec,

It is stated that the Dan'd Arundle on visiting the French court at the Great Exhibition was dogged from spot to spot by a French detective, who took down the name of every exhibitor at whose stall the royal party lingered

We understand that a memorial is about to be presented to her Majesty to allow the State apartments at Windsor Castle to be thrown open to the public, in anticipation of Windsor being visited by numerous foreigners during the Exhibition.

Thus far the Great Exhibition in London has been perfectly successful in a pecuniary sense The amount received for season tickets to the 9 th inst was 459, 649, Crowds of delighted and wondering daily congregate about the American sewing machines watching the operators.

France.

Murphy the famous Irish giant has just died of small-pox at Marseilles,

The Emperor Napoleon is attending the Paris spring races,

The *Moniteur* announced the departure of Prince Napoleon to Naples adds he has no political mission,

---

It is reported in Paris that the Emperor of China intends sending an embassy extraordinary to France and England,

The Emperor and Empress and the Queen of Holland honored the Gymnase Theatre, Paris, with their presence to see Mr Sarnou's new peice of La Perla Noire,

Local Intellegence,

There is great excitement in Montreal over an attempt to reduce the current value of the British shilling to 24s, The newspapers are reaping lists of retailers who will, and those who wont agree to the resolution.

Information wanted–Mr W. McSweeney while in Port Huron or Fort Gartiot a few days ago met in with a few of his old cronys, and very kindly invited them to partake of a 'ttle John' Barley Corn, they did so, and were 'unco happy ' which however termenated in a little fuss that ended,' Billy went to bed, and on getting up in the morning, his repeater, and all the loose Bank notes were gone, much to Billys discomfiture, any information respecting either, will be gladly received by him,

We would say to Mr McSweeney, the only cure for the above is to use one quart la'd of John Barley Corn, each time you and friends meet and in the course of a few weeks, the nett gain will more than remunerate for the loss, Ed H

Oil—We learn that a combination is being entered into by the Canada Oil well diggers, with a view of raising the price of the crude Oil, to a remuncritive figure, a very necessary move, as the difference between the prices of crude and refined

Continued on 2d page.

This newspaper is believed to be the only surviving copy of the *Herald*. Published by the young "Tom Edison" while working on the Grand Trunk Railroad running between Detroit and Port Huron, it was the first newspaper to be printed on a moving train.

Orville Wright made the world's first powered flight on December 17, 1903, in the airplane he and his brother, Wilbur, built in this bicycle shop at Dayton, Ohio. The shop now is in Greenfield Village. Their basic experiments began with the air-pressure test bicycle, left, which, when peddled rapidly, produced the effect of wind on the test vanes of the horizontal balance wheel. This device led to their conception and use of the first wind tunnel for obtaining data for designing their airplane. The wind tunnel is now a basic tool for the industry. From fixed-wing aircraft, designs advanced to rotating airfoil machines. The Vought-Sikorsky VS-300, above, piloted by its designer, Igor Sikorsky, made the first helicopter flight September 14, 1939. It is the forerunner of a series of helicopters now used for rescue, combat, photographing, and other situations requiring hovering and vertical flight.

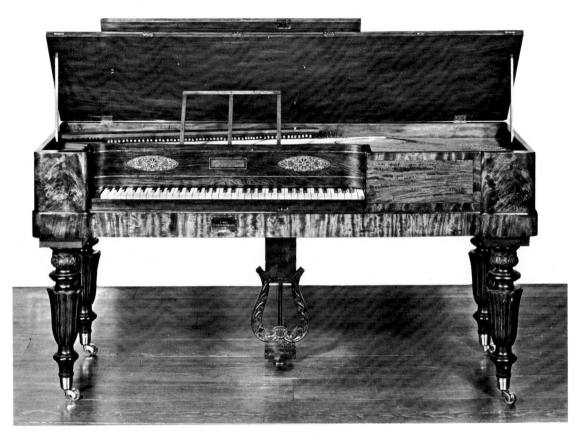

Jonas Chickering's first square piano was made in Boston, Massachusetts, in 1823.

Other Treasures not Illustrated

All non-illustrated entries in each category are listed approximately as they appear in the Museum's exhibit plan.

INDIAN SILVER GORGET AND PECTORAL — Made in Detroit by the unknown maker, "I M," *circa* 1720; these are the earliest known midwestern-made silver objects

BRASS BASS HORN — Played by James Hill and used in the first American brass band, Boston, Mass., 1835

1914 TRACTOR — The first production model manufactured by the Allis-Chalmers Company

1917 TRACTOR — The first production version manufactured by the Fordson Company

STEAM ENGINE — James Watt double-acting Sun and Planet Engine, the first to utilize parallel motion and flyball governor assembly, 1788

SUPER HETERODYNE RADIO — The first self-contained portable invented and made by Edwin Armstrong, *circa* 1922

SCREW-CUTTING LATHE — Made by Joseph Whitworth in the shop of Henry Mandeslay, Lambeth, England, *circa* 1828, the first lathe to achieve a uniform cutting thread

CORLISS ENGINE — Original George Corliss straight-line proportional intake valve steam engine, *circa* 1859; very few of these engines exist today

DECORATED HOUSE WAGON — Used in the late 19th century by King Steve, the first Gypsy King in California

1903 PACKARD "OLD PACIFIC" — First car to cross the United States entirely under its own power

1913 FORD TOURING CAR — First model to be built on a moving assembly line, which revolutionized *all* manufacturing

1932 FORD CABRIOLET — First mass-produced low cost *enbloc* V-8 engine automobile

1914 FRUEHAUF TRAILER — First commercially built trailer in the United States

1915 GASOLINE STATION — The first visible gasoline pumping station in the United States, made by the Raymond Garage Equipment Company, Adrian, Michigan

TRAFFIC SIGNAL — The world's first three-color, four-direction lamp, designed by W. L. Potts, Detroit, Michigan, 1920

1927 FORD RADIO RANGE STATION — The first successful airplane guidance system

AERONAUTIC COLLECTION FIRSTS —
    Flight over the North Pole — 1926 Fokker Tri-Motor
    Scheduled transcontinental passenger service — 1927 Boeing 40-B
    Flight over the Atlantic Ocean westwardly — 1927 Junkers
    Flight over the South Pole — 1928 Ford Tri-Motor
    Flight with diesel power — 1928 Stinson
    American Commercial Autogiro — 1931 Pitcairn
    First Successful plane with retractable landing gear and variable wing camber — 1920 Baumann "RB-Racer"

COLORED WOODCUT *MAP OF AMERICA* BY SEBASTIAN MUNSTER — The earliest map of the New World, 1550

THE HOLY BIBLE — Published in 1743 by Christoph Saur, first Bible to be printed in America in a European language

1896 DURYEA MOTOR WAGON COMPANY CATALOG — First promotion booklet for automobile company

COLLECTION OF DOCUMENTS — Established Henry Ford's position as the "father of mass production" utilizing the moving assembly line

ORIGINAL L.J.M. DAGUERRE PHOTOGRAPHIC OUTFIT — Complete with camera, tripod, fuming boxes and plate holder, *circa* 1845

DAGUERREOTYPE ET DU DIORAMA BY L.J.M. DAGUERRE, 1839 — The first publication introducing the art of photography based upon the Daguerre process

EDISON ELECTROHARMONIC TELEGRAPH — Quadruplex telegraphy, *circa* 1874

ORIGINAL EDISON EFFECT GALVANOMETER — *Circa* 1883, a device created by Thomas Edison by which he demonstrated his discovery of electricity passing from a filament to a plate in a vacuum; this was the basis for modern electronics

It was the financial success of Noah Webster's textbooks which enabled him in 1822 to build this handsome Federal style house at Temple and Grove Streets in New Haven, Connecticut. In the second floor front room at the left, he finished his *American Dictionary of the English Language* in 1828.

Historical Association Items

Along the main street, in the residential area of Greenfield Village, there stands a series of houses once occupied by America's doers: the Noah Webster House, dating from 1822; the Stephen Foster birthplace; the birthplace of William Holmes McGuffey, pioneer educator and author of the *McGuffey Eclectic Readers;* and the birthplace of Luther Burbank.

Facing the shaded Village Green is the Logan County, Illinois, Courthouse, where Abe Lincoln practiced law. Nearby is the Menlo Park Compound, comprised of Thomas A. Edison's office and library, his research laboratory, and supporting buildings.

Nearer the entrance to the Village is the Heinz House, where the Henry J. Heinz Company had its beginnings in 1869; the Wright house, where Orville Wright was born in 1871; the Cycle Shop, where the Wright brothers experimented with aerodynamics and constructed the first airplane for flight at Kitty Hawk; and the white frame farmhouse, birthplace of Henry Ford.

In Greenfield Village is preserved the living history of how America lived, worked and thought. Here, in some one hundred homes, craft shops, factories and public buildings, is preserved the basic fabric of America from the 17th to the 20th centuries. The word preserved is used most deliberately, for America's re-creation of its past has taken any one or more of several paths. Most desirable is preservation; then restoration, reconstruction, and finally, conjectural reconstruction.

To *preserve* means to keep as is, to maintain the fabric of a building as it has developed over the life span of that structure to the present. To *restore* is to move the physical appearance of a standing building backwards to some important point in the past life of that structure. *Reconstruction* is the exact rebuilding, on its original site, of a structure which has disappeared or been destroyed. *Conjectural reconstruction* is sometimes a venture into the unknown, beyond research and the study of existing prototypes.

Within these four categories, Greenfield Village represents, mainly, a preservation of examples of America's past, brought together at one geographical location.

The Henry Ford Museum, by contrast, is one great and vast structure housing collections of the American fine and decorative arts, crafts, tools and home industries, as well as agriculture, power, lighting, communications and transportation. There are the Ford Archives where many of the items are associated with historic personages of the 20th century. There are also collections of rare books, original manuscripts, company records of early American manufacturers and significant maps, prints and photographs in the Museum's Research Library.

The rich collections housed in Greenfield Village and the Henry Ford Museum represent collecting achievement in five distinct areas: Outstanding Firsts; Historical Association Items, Masterpieces of Craftsmanship, Unique Examples of artistic or inventive genius; World's Largest Collections.

Commander-in-Chief of the Revolutionary Army, first President of the United States, the "Father of His Country" — George Washington, left, is beyond doubt the most honored person ever associated with America. Almost any item he ever touched, or any house he ever visited, is today revered for his association. The objects, here shown, are more important than most Washingtonia, being directly connected to his everyday life.

The watercolor drawing, shown below, depicts the carriage used by George Washington at his first inaugural held in New York City in 1789. Built in London sometime prior to this date, it was then brought to the United States and redecorated, presumably because no suitably fashionable vehicle was available in the New York area. Besides this association, the drawing is one of the few such representations of an elegant coach extant today.

Profile of the Carriage of George Washington made in London

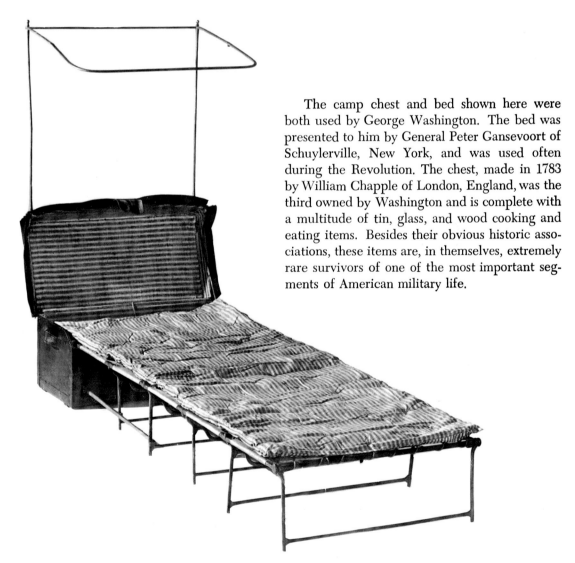

The camp chest and bed shown here were both used by George Washington. The bed was presented to him by General Peter Gansevoort of Schuylerville, New York, and was used often during the Revolution. The chest, made in 1783 by William Chapple of London, England, was the third owned by Washington and is complete with a multitude of tin, glass, and wood cooking and eating items. Besides their obvious historic associations, these items are, in themselves, extremely rare survivors of one of the most important segments of American military life.

Alexander Gardner's famous photograph of Abraham Lincoln pictures him sitting in an identical chair, as seen opposite. This photo was made at Washington, D.C., in 1863.

The Victorian rocker, on the left, is the chair in which Abraham Lincoln was seated at Ford's Theater, Washington, D.C., when John Wilkes Booth assassinated him in 1865. The Victorian armchair, above, stamped by Bembe & Kimmel of New York City, was one of the chairs made for the House of Representatives in 1857. In 1859 the chairs were determined to be too heavy and, as a result, several were sold at public auction. At least three were purchased for use in the photographic studios of Matthew Brady and Alexander Gardner. There are existing photographs of many notable people seated in these chairs, including Thaddeus Stevens, Andrew Johnson, James Garfield, as well as Lincoln.

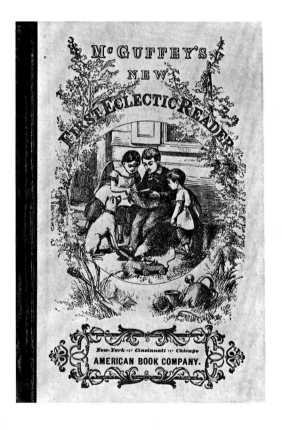

Stephen Foster was one of America's foremost composers of popular music. He arranged and played many of his famous songs on this historic guitar. Foster songs which are still favorites today include, "Old Dog Tray," "Old Black Joe," "Oh Susanna," "Beautiful Dreamer" and "Old Folks at Home." In the Museum Library are original manuscripts of two of Foster's songs — "Open Thy Lattice Love," composed when he was only sixteen years of age, and "Come Where My Love Lies Dreaming." In Greenfield Village, Foster's flute and flageolet are exhibited in his birthplace.

Although William Holmes McGuffey, who was born in Pennsylvania in 1800, was an educator and Presbyterian minister, he is best remembered as the author of the group of text books, the *Eclectic Readers,* published for the first six grades. Millions of Americans, including men like Henry Ford and the Wright brothers, used the famed books of which over 12 million were published. Shown left, from the Museum's complete collection of Readers, is McGuffey's *First* and *Second Reader* published in 1837 and 1838, respectively. It is interesting to note that in the past few years, many modern educators have advocated a return to these simple, well-written texts.

When Deming Jarves, the founder of the Boston and Sandwich Glass Company left that company in 1858, these engraved table pieces were among the gifts from his employees. Of brilliant clear cut glass, they are decorated with vintage designs on alternate panels, and each bears a "J" within a wreath. This group reached the Museum through the ownership of a Jarves granddaughter. The Sandwich Glass Plant in Greenfield Village was constructed with materials from the original Sandwich factory.

While not as graceful in form as the usual phaeton, this personal carriage of General Lafayette is unique in its three-wheel, light-weight design and is very comfortably supported on two elliptical transverse steel springs. It was built about 1820 and was brought from France in 1824 on the occasion of the second visit of the Marquis de Lafayette to America. He became ill and went to recuperate in the Verplanck homestead at Brinckerhoff, New York. During convalescence, Lafayette rode daily in this prized phaeton.

Among the most important orders for Chinese export porcelain was that placed by the Society of the Cincinnati for a dinner service which was destined for General Washington. The set, of about 300 pieces, was received in 1786, and bore on each piece the emblem of the Society held by the Angel of Fame, within a blue Fitzhugh border. It was used at Mount Vernon, and bequeathed by Washington to his step-grandson, George Washington Parke Custis. He in turn left it to his daughter, the wife of General Robert E. Lee, who lived at Arlington House, across the Potomac from the Capitol. Much of the service was destroyed during the Civil War.

The yellow cotton petticoat, glazed and quilted, is, by family tradition, part of the wedding garments of Deborah Read when she married Benjamin Franklin in 1730. The costume collection is one of several "iceberg" collections in the textile holdings of the Museum which deserves greater attention. Although 18th century garments are included, the bulk dates from 1825 to 1900. Garments are of interest not only for their design and materials, but also for the insight they give into past customs and ways of life. The millinery collection is represented by the basketweave ashwood hat worn by Jenny Lind during her concert tours in 1850.

In 1902, Henry Ford designed and built this pioneer racer dubbed "999" after a fast N.Y. Central locomotive. Driven by Barney Oldfield, "999" became world famous as a consistent race winner and record breaker. In 1904, Henry Ford personally drove "999" on the ice of Lake St. Clair to set a one mile record at 91.4 MPH. Its 1157 cu. in. engine is probably the largest four-cylinder automobile engine ever built.

The watch, made by Cartier of New York, *circa* 1925, and the frame, shown here, were the personal property of Henry Ford, the founder of this Institution. The watch is one of over 3500 horological items contained in the collections of the Museum. The photograph shows early portraits of Mr. and Mrs. Ford, their son Edsel and his wife Eleanor Clay, and their children Henry II, Benson, Josephine and William Clay.

White House Haviland porcelain state service ordered in 1861 by President Lincoln.

Other Treasures not Illustrated

All non-illustrated entries in each category are listed approximately as they appear in the Museum's exhibit plan.

FLEMISH-STYLE SIDE CHAIR — Made in New England, *circa* 1690-1710, and originally owned by Sir William and Lady Pepperell of Kittery, Maine

WILLIAM AND MARY HIGH CHEST OF DRAWERS — Made in New England, *circa* 1700-1720, and owned by Mary Ball Washington, the mother of George Washington

QUEEN ANNE SIDE CHAIR — Made in Philadelphia, Pennsylvania, *circa* 1760, by William Savery for Mrs. Savery's granddaughter and namesake, Mary

PAIR OF QUEEN ANNE SIDE CHAIRS — Made by Solomon Fussell at Philadelphia, Pennsylvania, *circa* 1750, for Benjamin Franklin

CHIPPENDALE CARD TABLE — Made in Massachusetts, *circa* 1760-1780, and owned by John Hancock, Signer of the Declaration of Independence

CHIPPENDALE SIDE CHAIR — Made at Salem, Massachusetts, *circa* 1770, and lent to George Washington for his use at Cambridge, Massachusetts, by the Honorable William Greenleaf of Boston, July 1775

HEPPLEWHITE SIDE CHAIR — Owned by Elias Hasket Derby (1739-1799), the Salem, Massachusetts, merchant and ship-owner

EMPIRE BREAKFRONT-DESK — Made by Joseph Barry of Philadelphia, Pa., *circa* 1810, for Andrew Jackson

VICTORIAN PARLOR SUITE — Made by John Henry Belter of New York, *circa* 1850, and used by Abraham Lincoln in his Springfield, Illinois, home

THEATER PROGRAM AND WOOL SHAWL — April 14, 1865, handbill for *Our American Cousin* and shawl used by Abraham Lincoln the night he was assassinated

BANJO CLOCK — Made in New England, *circa* 1815, and owned by both Robert Morris and General John Stark

PORCELAIN PLATES — Set of six "Mississippi Bubble" plates decorated with satirical sketches referring to the failure of John Law's attempt to found a settlement in Mississippi; Ching-te-Chen, China, *circa* 1720

BEVERAGE SET — Meissen porcelain, *circa* 1810, owned by President John Adams

CUT GLASS PUNCH BOWL — Made in Pittsburgh, Pennsylvania, *circa* 1820-1825, and owned by Robert Morris, Signer of the Declaration of Independence

GLASS PAPERWEIGHT — Made at the Boston and Sandwich Glass Company, Sandwich, Massachusetts, and used by Abraham Lincoln

GOLD WEDDING RING — Used at the marriage ceremony of William Henry Stiegel and Elizabeth Holtz in Roxborough, Pennsylvania, October 24, 1758

SILVER CAUDLE CUP — Made, *circa* 1670, by Jeremiah Dummer for Mary Hollingsworth, a victim of the Salem witchcraft trials

SILVER SALVER — The only known object bearing the marks of both Myer Myers and of his partnership with Benjamin Halsted, 1763-1764; made for Charity Johnson, wife of the first President of what is now Columbia University, New York

SILVER TANKARD — Made by Peter Van Dyck, New York, *circa* 1710, and engraved, *circa* 1813, by James D. Stout with the coat-of-arms of John Pintard, founder of the New-York-Historical Society in 1804

SILVER TEA SET — Made by Charters, Cann and Dunn, New York, *circa* 1850, and used by President James K. Polk

SILVER TROWEL — Made by Francis W. Cooper and used in laying the cornerstone of Tammany Hall, New York City, 1867

WOOD SCULPTURE OF MAN SUPPORTING AN EAGLE — Presented by the sculptor E. A. McKillop of Balfour, North Carolina, to Henry Ford, February 11, 1929

COMPLETE SHEET OF TWO-CENT STAMPS — Issued in commemoration of the 50th Anniversary of the Invention of the Electric Light; signed and dated by Thomas Edison, December 5, 1929

LUTHER BURBANK'S SPADE — Used by Thomas Edison at the laying of the cornerstone of the Henry Ford Museum, September 27, 1928

1907 EXPERIMENTAL TRACTOR — The version built by Henry Ford, based on Model B and K Ford automobiles

GLASSMAKERS TOOLS — Used by Ralph Barber, Vineland, New Jersey, in making "Millville Rose" paperweights, *circa* 1910

WORK BENCH — Used by the early betty lamp manufacturer, Peter Derr, at Bernville, Pennsylvania, mid-19th century

HISTORIC AUTOMOBILES — 1923 Lincoln and 1928 Ford "A", number 1, given by Henry Ford to his friend Thomas Edison; 1932 Chrysler, custom-built for Walter P. Chrysler, founder of the Chrysler Corporation; 1939 Lincoln used by King George VI and Queen Elizabeth II on their American and Canadian tours; 1940 Chrysler, New York City Parade Car, used for nearly 20 years to drive world dignitaries

PRESIDENTIAL VEHICLES — 1902 Brougham used by President Theodore Roosevelt; 1912 Baker Electric Car used by Presidents Taft, Wilson, Harding and Coolidge; 1939 Lincoln used by Presidents Roosevelt and Truman; 1950 Lincoln used by Presidents Truman, Eisenhower, Kennedy and Johnson

1919 EXCELSIOR MOTORCYCLE — Owned by Charles A. Lindbergh

1929 LOCKHEED VEGA AIRPLANE — Used by Donald MacMillan on his arctic explorations and by Billy Mitchell, Wiley Post, Amelia Earhart and Charles Lindbergh

BOOKPLATE — Printed for George Washington, *circa* 1770

POWDER HORN — Used in a military engagement off the coast of Cuba in 1762, the last foreign battle in which Americans served under the British Flag

HOLOGRAPH LETTERS — Written by George Washington, Marquis de Lafayette, Thomas Jefferson, Dolly Madison, James Madison, John Quincy Adams, John Hancock, Noah Webster, Abraham Lincoln, Thomas Edison and James Fenimore Cooper, as well as many others written by noted Americans

HOLOGRAPH MANUSCRIPT — The four verses of *America* signed by the author Samuel Francis Smith, 1832

AUTOGRAPHED PHOTOGRAPH OF STEPHEN FOSTER — *Circa* 1846

MANUSCRIPT COPY OF THE THIRTEENTH AMENDMENT TO THE CONSTITUTION — Signed by Abraham Lincoln, 1865

PHOTOGRAPH OF THOMAS A. EDISON AND HIS STAFF — Interior of the Edison Laboratory, Menlo Park, New Jersey, February 22, 1880

DAGUERREOTYPE — An early picture of George Corliss and his family

TELEGRAPH TABLE — Edison's personal table which is now in the Edison Laboratory at Menlo Park in Greenfield Village; he used this piece of furniture from the age of 15

Rococo silver coffee pot made by Paul Revere (1735-1818), Boston, Massachusetts, *circa* 1760.

Masterpieces
of
Craftsmanship

Until the 19th Century, the traditional craftsman's training was the apprenticeship system. A youth in his early teens was bound out by his parents to work for a "master" craftsman, for a stipulated period of years, to learn that artisan's trade. To be sure, he had household tasks and duties, but he gradually learned the elements of his craft, plus the reading, writing, and arithmetic necessary to keep accurate accounts and to render bills.

Completing his apprenticeship, the young craftsman became a journeyman — a craftsman who hired himself out to earn wages and to save for the opening of his own shop. Eventually, after acquiring working experience and the full development of technical and design skills, he might become a master craftsman. In Europe, to cross the boundary between journeyman and master, he was often required to make a *set piece*—his masterpiece. This indicated to all, and particularly his peers and potential clients, his abilities within the discipline of his craft.

The masterpieces shown in the Henry Ford Museum are really not *set pieces*. Rather, they are the flowering of the craftsman's genius, be he potter, cabinet-maker, pewterer, gunsmith, or silversmith.

A superb example in this category is the crisply carved Queen Anne desk and bookcase, in cherry, made in Connecticut between 1750 and 1780. An equivalent is the officer's pistol, fashioned by J. Welschans of York, Pennsylvania, ca. 1780, the only known American pistol of such early date decorated with silver wire; the four Cremona violins: one by Amati, two by Stradivari, and one by Guarnerius, and the accompanying bow by Xavier Tourte of Paris, France.

Equally important are examples not included in the Selected Treasures display area: the superb wood-paneled interior of the World War I Joswin automobile; furniture by Townsend, Seymour, McIntire, Phyfe, Lannuier, automotive brass lamps and horns, engravings, frakturs, books. There is silver, pewter, glass. There are lamps, tools, textiles. Literally, it is impossible to walk the corridors of the museum without seeing craft masterpieces in every glance at cases or standing objects.

In no way was craftsmanship destroyed by the Industrial Revolution. For a time, craft skills were eclipsed as factories took shape and machines took over the work of the human hand. The inventive skill of the craftsman has survived, however. No better example exists than the sculpture-like Bugatti "Royale," ca. 1930, the biggest, heaviest, most beautiful automobile the world has ever seen.

Traditional American craft processes are carried on even to this day in Greenfield Village. A silversmith raises a bowl or cuts a bracelet. Potters work at the wheel. Spinners spin. Weavers throw their shuttles across their warp threads. A blacksmith forges hinges and implements of wrought iron. A rug-maker hooks his 19th Century patterns. Crafts and craft techniques live on, a reminder of America's past, a promise that personal product qualities will not cease.

The six-panel drinking-bowl, shown above, and the set of Apostle spoons, shown right, are both of artistic and historic significance. The bowl, by Jesse Kip (1660-1722), is a typical early New York form and was presented to Jacob and Maria Van Dorn in 1699, on the occasion of their colt winning a one-mile race on the King's Highway at Middletown, New Jersey. This bowl, with two cast caryatid handles, is the earliest known American racing trophy that retains its original form. The complete set of James I Apostle spoons, known as the Sulhamstead set, by the unknown maker "IS" London, 1617-1618, is one of only five sets known made by a single maker within the same year. The gilded figures on the spoons show the Apostolic emblems according to the Germanic system and include in the nimbus of each, a dove, symbolic of the Holy Ghost.

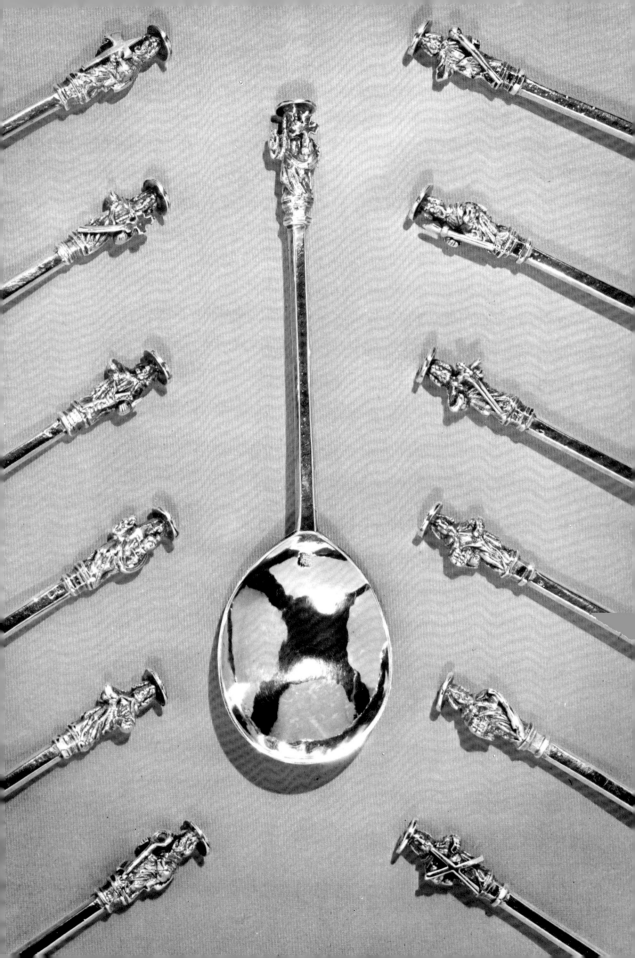

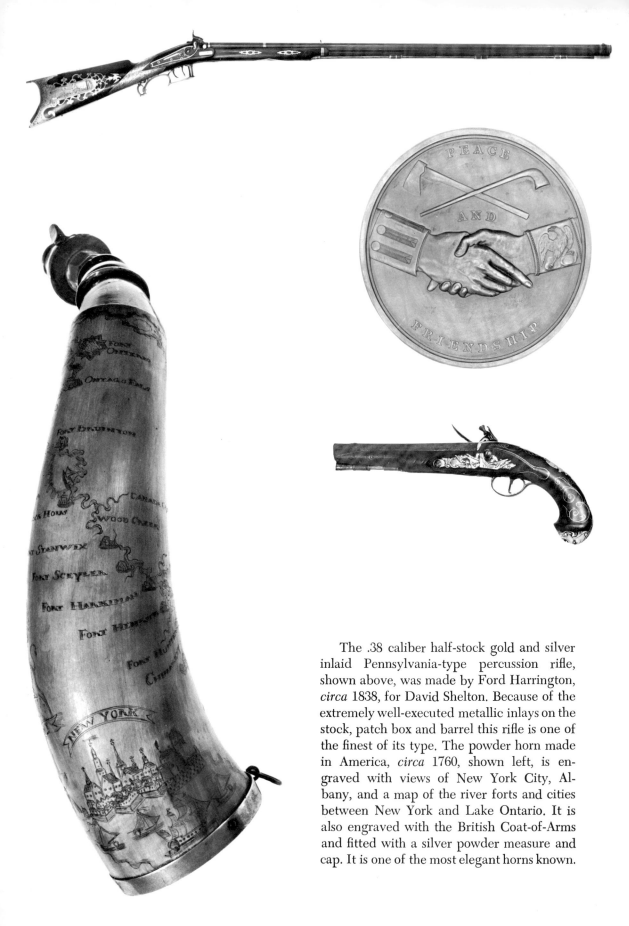

The .38 caliber half-stock gold and silver inlaid Pennsylvania-type percussion rifle, shown above, was made by Ford Harrington, *circa* 1838, for David Shelton. Because of the extremely well-executed metallic inlays on the stock, patch box and barrel this rifle is one of the finest of its type. The powder horn made in America, *circa* 1760, shown left, is engraved with views of New York City, Albany, and a map of the river forts and cities between New York and Lake Ontario. It is also engraved with the British Coat-of-Arms and fitted with a silver powder measure and cap. It is one of the most elegant horns known.

The silver Indian peace medal, shown left, was designed by John Reich and was struck by the U. S. Government at Philadelphia in 1801. Shown on the obverse is a bust of Thomas Jefferson, and on the reverse, two clasped hands with crossed tomahawk and calumet inscribed: "Peace and Friendship." Medals of this type were struck during the administration of each of our early Presidents and were intended as gifts of friendship from the United States Government to prominent Indian Chiefs.

The Pennsylvania flintlock, English-style Officer's pistol, shown lower left, is marked on the barrel: "Yorktown IF" and on the lock plate: "J. Welschans." It has a walnut stock with silver wire inlay on the grips and a silver mask butt plate. The silver work was probably executed by John Ford, known to have worked in York, Pennsylvania, *circa* 1780. This piece is considered to be the finest and most important American pistol known today, and is the only extant example of this type having silver wire inlay.

Among this Museum's extensive collection of eighteenth century wrought iron is the candle trammel, shown right. It was made in Pennsylvania in the mid-seventeen hundreds. Ordinary household objects were very often given decorative motifs, although not usually as extensively or as delicately ornamented as this trammel. The large rooster, the several decorative hearts and the acorn finial on the rachet handle are most skillfully crafted. This functional piece is well designed, both artistically and mechanically. It surely was treasured by its original owner as much as it is today by connoisseurs of American art.

The German immigrants to Colonial America of course brought with them their traditional designs and techniques. Illustrated above are two examples of North Carolina redware with slip decoration made by the Moravians, and two from Pennsylvania with sgraffito decoration.

The pottery at Bethabara, North Carolina, began operation about 1757, and was succeeded by the pottery at Salem about ten years later. The large jar with its fitted cover, which so handsomely completes the outline, is a "sugar jar," and has bands of black, white, and pea-green slip which show in colorful contrast to the red of the body. The large plate is almost completely covered with slip, a dark chocolate brown for the ground, with the border and the bird-on-a-branch motif done in cream and custard colors. The ease with which this difficult slipware technique is handled suggests a master's hand. The casual-seeming decoration pleasingly enhances the surfaces of these large pieces.

Unlike the Carolina Moravians, the German potters of Pennsylvania utilized both slip and sgraffito (or scratched) decoration. The two-handled jar has an intricate design of tulips and a peafowl worked beneath an elaborate "canopy." The inscription has been translated: "Today is the day I will not lend; anyone who wants to borrow must come again tomorrow." George Huebner, who worked in Montgomery County during the last quarter of the 18th century, undoubtedly created this outstanding piece.

The other illustrated example is the interior view of a small barber basin by the Bucks County potter, David Spinner. Here a delicate scratched outline has been filled with colored slips over a cream-colored ground. The inscription reads: "By everything in the world I know not why my beard has grown so thin 1791."

The ceramic collection also contains fine examples by other Pennsylvania German potters, notably Andrew Headman, John Nase, Jacob Medinger, Willoughby Smith as well as members of the Bell family, Anthony Baecher, Jacob Eberly, and many others.

The stamped markings on this stoneware jug indicate that it was made at Hartford, Connecticut, by Daniel Goodale, Jr., for Levi Stewart. The incised decoration is an unusual design and the use of an American frigate (perhaps the *Constitution*) suggests a possible date of 1830.

The contrast between this utilitarian redware wash bowl and water pitcher, and the highly-ornamneted stoneware jug is remarkable. They were all made in Tuscarawas County, Ohio, and are dated 1840 and 1858, respectively. The bowl and pitcher were produced at Zoar, Ohio, and the bowl is dated 1840. The stoneware jug, with its matching stopper, is signed three times: "E. Hall," and obviously was intended to prove Hall's artistic and technical ability. Ornamented with stamped and applied decoration, and highlighted with light and deep blue glaze, Hall utilized a saddled horse, clasped hands, and tulip plants in the design. The strongly modeled handle appears to be held in place by straps and screws, all represented in clay.

Left is one of a pair of pistol-handled Chinese Export porcelain urns which once belonged to the Winthrop family of Boston, Massachusetts, *circa* 1785. On marbleized bases, they have blue and gold floral decoration, two bands of gold stars on a blue ground, a ribbon band about the shaft, and a finial in the shape of an artichoke. The identical sepia landscape scenes are framed in blue and gold, and placed within a blue and gilt swag of stylized high relief cicadas. In addition to the handsome design and the historical importance of these urns, they are the tallest recorded, being 26⅜ inches in height. Although the made-to-order porcelains exported by the Chinese were not of the same high qualtiy as those kept for their own use and admiration, they were eagerly acquired by both Americans and Europeans. The long wait necessitated by sending the order by ship to Canton, the time required for manufacture in Ching-te-Chen, and the delivery of the finished pieces added not only to their value but to their exotic appeal.

This salt-glazed stoneware punch pot is of imposing height (9½ inches), and ornamented with brilliant polychromed floral decoration in large and small shell-edged shaped reserves on the pink enamelled body. It is one of the extremely rare forms of Staffordshire pottery, and dates from the third quarter of the eighteenth century. The bail handle is fixed in place, and the cover is topped by a bird finial.

The red tole coffee pot, shown right, was made in Eastern Pennsylvania, *circa* 1825. It is one of the few pieces of its type fully documented. The original maker, price and owner are inscribed on the bottom: "James Fulivier 75CTs is the price of this," and: "Jared H. Young." Although Mr. Fulivier is otherwise unknown, this one object alone is sufficient to place him in the forefront of the tinsmiths of his era. Beautifully decorated, it is one of the most outstanding examples of American tole work known today.

Since the mid-18th century, Staffordshire has been the major pottery-making center of England. Among the most colorful wares are those produced about 1820 and referred to as "Gaudy Dutch." Perhaps the most popular of the many floral patterns is the "Single Rose" design, depicted on this utilitarian and well-used deep bowl. The red and blue decoration, emphasized with yellow and green, is held within a blue and yellow border. Note the rather restrained floral spray on the underside.

This unique secretary-desk and bookcase-on-frame bridges the gap between the seventeenth century and the Queen Anne styles. The carved leafage with punched ground is reminiscent of carving found on seventeenth century chests and on numerous doorways throughout the Connecticut River Valley. The pad foot and arched panels are typical of the Queen Anne period. Made in three sections, this piece dates *circa* 1750-1780. Initials carved below the bonnet are as yet unidentified. See detail on left.

Illustrated are a few of the outstanding violins in the Henry Ford Museum collection. The violin on the right was made by Nicola Amati in 1647 and is the earliest example in the collection. The two center violins are products of the workshop of Antonio Stradivari made in 1709 and 1703, respectively. Far left is "The Doyen" made by Joseph Guarnerius del Gesu in 1741. All were made in Cremona, Italy, and all still retain the magnificent tone which made them so desirable to musicians in the seventeenth and eighteenth centuries.

The Communal Society of Shakers was started in America by Mother Ann Lee in 1776. They were known as "Believers." Their philosophy was based upon a oneness with Christ, a pure and celibate life, common ownership of property, and abstinence from evil. The beauty and simplicity of Shaker design and its perfection of craftsmanship, is apparent in these oval boxes. The basic theory of practical utility with a degree of comfort and a lack of superfluous decoration, is typical of all Shaker-made products. The Museum collection includes Shaker furniture for home and shop, textiles, metal-work, tools and baskets.

This colorful fraktur certificate commemorates the marriage of Francis Stanger and Elizabeth L. Campbell, March 11, 1803. While it would be considered desirable either for its beautiful design or for the rarity of New Jersey certificates, it has an historical association that overrides these considerations. The Stanger family, of which Francis was a member, were the founders, in 1781, of the second glass house in New Jersey. It lasted under varied ownership until 1824. Francis also may have been associated with the earliest New Jersey glass factory, that of John Frederick Amelung, as a bottle, easily attributable to this plant, inscribed: "F. Stenger"(sic), was handed down along with this certificate in the Stanger family.

Denis Diderot (1713-1784), a French philosopher and writer, spent more than twenty years compiling this monumental encyclopaedia. It consisted of twenty-eight volumes and eight supplements. Although prominent men such as Voltaire and Rousseau contributed to the work, Diderot wrote several hundred articles, including all those on technology and industry, as well as many dealing with philosophy and science. A treasure of the engraver's art, these pages, as may be seen right, give a thorough presentation of the various crafts and sciences as they were practiced during Diderot's lifetime, along with details regarding such diversified material as fishing and architecture. Although it was originally intended to spread technical and philosophical knowledge throughout the Old World, it now serves the historian as a prime source of information on early crafts and production methods.

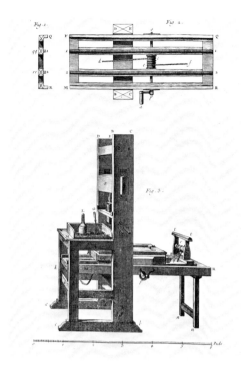

The first edition of the King James Bible, shown right, was completed by a group of fifty-four leading English clergymen in 1611. Although famed in its day for excellent scholarship, it is equally revered today for the quality of its printing and wonderfully decorative design. It is interesting to note that numerous adaptations of the decorative motif, shown below, taken from the Book of Job, are found on a series of painted chests originating in Guilford and Saybrook, Connecticut, *circa* 1690-1720.

The important silver tankard, shown left, is an early example of the basic form of tankards from the New York area. Two craftsmen were involved in its construction — Cornelius Kierstede (1674-1757), who fashioned the body, *circa* 1700, and Philip Goelet (1708-1748), who added the cover, *circa* 1725. The engraving on the piece is especially well executed, as is the cutcard base-band and the handle decoration. Less heavily decorated, but equally elegant, the pewter tankard, shown below, by Frederick Bassett (1740-1800), New York, *circa* 1780, is obviously related in design to its earlier silver counterpart. Here again, the lip, handle and baseband are set off by a plain tapering body. Frederick's father, John (1696-1761), was also a pewterer and the 6⅝ inch beaker, shown here, is attributed to him. It was made in New York, *circa* 1740, and although it is very plain, its early date and large size make it extremely rare.

This Wedgwood plaque, "The Apotheosis of Virgil," is matched in the Museum's collection with a companion panel, "The Apotheosis of Homer." The designs were modeled by Flaxman, made about 1785, and bear the impressed "Wedgwood" mark. Plaques, varying in size from tiny pieces for jewelry to these 24-inch ones, were much in demand. The large ones were often framed in architectural panelling, mounted in fireplace mantels or used on furniture.

Ettore Bugatti, artistic creator of dramatic sports cars in Molsheim, France, demonstrated his versatility by building six magnificent Type 41 "Royales" between 1927 and 1932; all survive. Each was designed to be of such size and elegance that it would shame every other pretentious classic car. This Bugatti, built in 1930 for Dr. Joseph Fuchs, was fitted with a custom body by Ludwig Weinberger in Munich. Charles Chayne acquired it in 1940 and restored it. The 784 cu. in. eight-cylinder engine will drive the "Royale" up to 125 miles per hour.

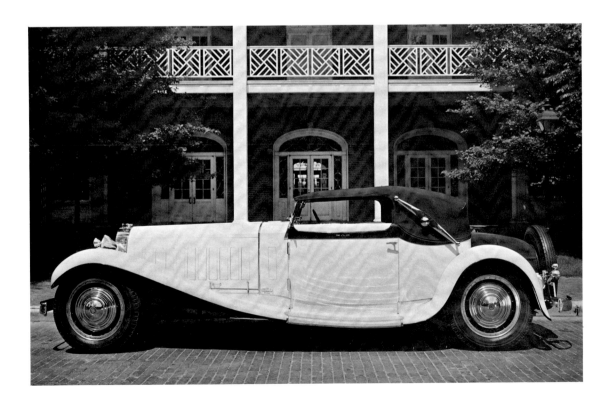

The portrait of Major General Henry Dearborn (1751-1829), shown right, was painted by the artist, Gilbert Stuart (1755-1828), at Boston, Massachusetts, *circa* 1810-1815. Dearborn was Secretary of War during the presidency of Thomas Jefferson and later Commander of the Northern Army of the United States. He was honored by the residents of the present City of Dearborn, Michigan, who renamed their town for him, although he is not known to have spent any great length of time here. Gilbert Stuart is generally recognized as one of the foremost artists in America. He achieved recognition in England and Ireland, where he worked for fifteen years. This portrait is of the subject at the height of his military career. He is wearing the prized badge of the Order of the Cincinnati.

Other Treasures not Illustrated

All non-illustrated entries in each category are listed approximately as they appear in the Museum's exhibit plan.

WILLIAM AND MARY DRESSING TABLE — Made in Philadelphia, Pa., *circa* 1700-1720, in tiger maple

PHILADELPHIA QUEEN ANNE SIDE CHAIR — With balloon seat and crest, centered by carved shells, made for the Caleb Pusey family

PHILADELPHIA CHIPPENDALE MAHOGANY CARD TABLE—Gadrooned serpentine apron, beaded drawer, pierced brackets and cable-molded legs made by Thomas Affleck

CHIPPENDALE EASY CHAIR — Made in Philadelphia, Pennsylvania, *circa* 1760-1775, by Benjamin Randolph

SCHRANK — Boldly-painted floral motifs and marbleizing on this sturdy utilitarian wardrobe are the epitome of Pennsylvania German decoration, Lancaster County, *circa* 1790

INLAID HEPPLEWHITE SECRETARY-DESK AND BOOKCASE — Made by John Seymour of Boston, *circa* 1800

PORCELAIN VASE — Made by Edward Lycett at the Faience Manufacturing Company, Greenpoint, N.Y., 1889

BLOWN COVERED SUGAR BOWL — With red and blue loops, made by Nicholas Lutz at the Boston and Sandwich Glass Company, Sandwich, Massachusetts, *circa* 1870

CLEAR GLASS COVERED PUNCH BOWL AND EIGHT CANDLESTICKS — Made by the Steuben Glass Company, Corning, New York

SILVER CRUET STAND — Made by Joseph and Nathaniel Richardson for General John Cadwalader, Philadelphia, Pennsylvania, *circa* 1771

SILVER EWER — Made by Myer Myers, New York, *circa* 1760

CORAL AND GOLD RATTLE — Made by William Faris, Annapolis, Maryland, *circa* 1765

GOLD WASHED SILVER COFFEE SERVICE — Made by Edwin Stebbins & Company, New York, *circa* 1850

3½ PINT PEWTER TANKARD — Made by Francis Bassett I, New York, before 1740

PINT PEWTER TANKARD — Made by Frederick Bassett, New York, *circa* 1780

PEWTER COMMUNION SERVICE — A 23-piece service made by Thomas Danforth Boardman, Hartford, Connecticut, *circa* 1825

BRONZE MOLD FOR A PEWTER PLATE — Set in an iron frame, signed "J S, 1826"

PLASTER BUSTS OF BENJAMIN FRANKLIN AND GEORGE WASHINGTON — Modeled by the French sculptor, Jean Antoine Houdon, *circa* 1770

MARBLE BUST OF JAMES McMILLAN — United States Senator from Michigan, 1889-1902, carved by Augustus St. Gaudens

BRONZE FIGURAL GROUP ENTITLED "THE RATTLESNAKE" — Modeled by Frederick Remington (1861-1909), and cast by the Roman Bronze Works

OIL PORTRAIT OF AN UNKNOWN MAN — Painted by Joseph Badger, Boston, Massachusetts, *circa* 1750

OIL PORTRAIT OF JOHN DUNCAN — Painted by Thomas McIlworth, New York, *circa* 1760

OIL PORTRAIT OF RALPH IZARD — Painted by Jeremiah Theus, Charleston, South Carolina, *circa* 1765

MINIATURE PORTRAIT OF THOMAS L. FERGUSON — Painted on ivory by Charles Wilson Peale, Philadelphia, Pennsylvania, *circa* 1790

OIL PORTRAIT OF WILLIAM MOORE — Painted by Charles Peale Polk, Baltimore, Md., 1793

TROMPE L'OEIL PORTRAIT OF AN UNKNOWN GIRL — Painted by George Washington Mark, Greenfield, Connecticut, *circa* 1845

CIGAR STORE INDIAN — Wooden figure called "Seneca John," carved by Arnold and Peter Ruef, father and son, Tiffin, Ohio, *circa* 1880

TALL-CASE CLOCK — Case carved by Thomas Affleck, Philadelphia, Pennsylvania, *circa* 1765

JAPANNED TALL-CASE CLOCK — Made by Gawen Brown, Boston, Massachusetts, 1766

AARON LANE TALL-CASE CLOCK — Case labeled by Ichabod Williams, later repaired by Joachim Hill; Elizabethtown, New Jersey, *circa* 1790

SHELF CLOCK — Made by Martin Cheney, Windsor, Vermont, *circa* 1790

PRESENTATION BANJO CLOCK — Made by Aaron Willard, Boston, Massachusetts, *circa* 1825

GIRANDOLE CLOCK — Made by Lemuel Curtis, Concord, Massachusetts, *circa* 1825

SILVER POCKET WATCH — Made by Gawen Brown, Boston, Massachusetts, *circa* 1775

POWDER HORN — Engraved by William Borbel with a map naming locations on the Pennsylvania Turnpike between Pittsburgh and Philadelphia, Pennsylvania, *circa* 1760

PAIR OF SILVER INLAID PISTOLS — Made by Peter White, Fayette County, Pennsylvania, *circa* 1820

SILVER INLAID KENTUCKY-TYPE RIFLE — Made by G. Scott, Coshocton, Ohio, *circa* 1830

TRACTION ENGINE — The style and perfection of design are outstanding in this machine made by the Avery Farm Machinery Company, Peoria, Illinois, 1916

UP-AND-DOWN PIT SAW — The finest known early example of this type of saw

CAST IRON SIX-PLATE STOVE — Made at Hampton Furnace, Frederick County, Maryland, *circa* 1760

CAST IRON GOTHIC STOVE — Made by Dr. Eliphalet Nott, Schenectady, New York, *circa* 1833

WALKING BEAM ENGINE — Gothic design made in 1836 and used until 1929 in the shop of John T. Lewis and Brothers, Philadelphia, Pennsylvania

PAIR OF CHANDELIERS — Carved and painted wood, with wire arms, New England, *circa* 1800

PEWTER CHANDELIER — Made by William S. Lawrence, Meriden, Connecticut with three decorated pewter fish fonts, mounted around his patented 1834 lard burner

KEROSENE LAMP 40½ INCHES HIGH — Overlay glass with bronze and marble mountings, and frosted cut shade with prisms, made by the Boston and Sandwich Glass Company, Sandwich, Massachusetts, *circa* 1880

1797 "CAMPBELL" CHARIOT — An outstanding example of construction, decoration and ornamentation, owned by Angelica Campbell and made by William Ross, New York

THE "NIAGARA" FIRE ENGINE — Hand pumper, built in 1797 and used at Plymouth, Massachusetts

1922 JOSWIN AUTOMOBILE — Interior inlaid in rosewood and mahogany with gold and ivory fittings

FIRST EDITION OF *THE BOOK OF MARTYRS* — Hand-produced by the Brothers of the Ephrata Cloisters in Pennsylvania, 1748-1749; the largest book printed in this country prior to the Revolution, containing the fraktur bookplate of Abraham Wohlgemuth

CATALOGUE OF CARRIAGE DESIGNS — Produced by Brewster and Company of Broom St., New York, 1879

Representing the world's largest collection of antique automobile accessories are this brass headlamp and snake-head bulb horn.

World's Largest Collections

To speak of having the world's largest collections in any category—be it buttons or silver spoons—can be an idle boast based on numerical superiority alone. It is quality and content that set a collection apart and make it worthy of attention and study.

Greenfield Village and the Henry Ford Museum house superb collections of lamps and lighting devices, American glass, coins and currency, alternating electric motors, walking-beam engines, clocks and watches, automotive parts (both European and American), Edisonia and transportation materials.

Indeed, in these listed areas, it can be said that the Village and the Museum collections of the above-enumerated items are among the world's largest, and that they have been developed carefully over the longer period to survey their fields in both quality and content.

What do these comprehensive collections mean to the viewer, whatever his interests may be? Here is study material in depth.

Transportation, for instance, includes not only steam, electric and gasoline automobiles, but the full range of wagons and carriages, sulkies and pony carts, sleighs, airplanes, bicycles, motorcycles, trucks, and buses. Here is the story of the development of locomotion in America.

In the sub-area of horse-drawn vehicles, there are illustrated the steps in advancement of design, construction, and efficiency. On exhibition is shown the colonial gig, the chaise and chair, the buckboard and the rockaway. There are coaches, hansom cabs, broughams, victorias, and landaus. There are surreys, breaks, buggies, phaetons, traps, and cabriolets.

Of particular interest are the everyday work vehicles: the heavy Conestoga wagon, the colorful American Railway Express wagon, the simple, box-like farm wagon, the multi-seated hotel bus, the stage, the dump wagon, the beer wagon, the horse ambulance, a kerosene tank wagon, a steam calliope and a hearse.

Many of these vehicle names mean little or nothing to the automobile-oriented citizen of today except as carriage names are carried over to new car models. But, for the interested, here are examples of carriage-making as the exacting craft it was: the selection and shaping of fine and durable woods, the development of springing for passenger comfort, tasteful ornamentation by painting and carving, and fine upholstery.

Custom carriages were not inexpensive. The Nevada Governor's coach was priced at $10,000. An 1800 wagonette cost $4,500. One of the hansom cabs, made *circa* 1880 in Chicago, sold for $2,500. These vehicles were comparable to today's range of automobiles.

The world's largest collections, when well conceived for comprehensive and orderly inclusion, create a self-importance not based on size. Theirs is a largeness of chronological survey, a fullness of story-line that cannot be duplicated elsewhere.

These three sugar bowls were selected to represent the collection of American glass. They illustrate three manufacturing techniques and three areas of glass production. The cover and body of the wisteria blown three-mold bowl, above left, were formed in the same mold. The fine ribs of the base reappear in the hollow finial of the cover. This piece was the expert manipulation of Frederick Mutzer, one of the few American glass workers whose name and products can be related. Because Mutzer worked at several New England glass houses between 1825 and 1835, the exact factory in which this sugar bowl was formed cannot be determined. The clear glass bowl, above right, pattern-molded, with a diamond-quilted design, is of unusual size, and has an applied base and tooled finial. Technique and style associate it with H. W. Stiegel's Lancaster Co., Pa., glass houses, although, it can only be called "Stiegel-type." The free-blown deep amber bowl, right, was made at the Ellenville Glass Works in Ulster County, New York, between 1836 and 1850.

Gallery E, which contains examples of the Museum's Empire and Victorian furniture, also houses eight wall cases with a major representation of American glass. Shown is the case of Midwestern glass, where globular bottles, pattern-molded ten-diamond pieces and other examples of "Ohio Stiegel" may be recognized, together with several choice examples from little-known Michigan factories.

The Washington press, shown above, has many literary, political, and personal associations, the most important of which is its connection with the inimitable American humorist, Mark Twain. Decorated with relief bust portraits of George Washington and Benjamin Franklin, it was manufactured by R. Hoe and Company at New York and purchased by Judge J. Judson Ames, prior to 1848. He took it to Baton Rouge, Louisiana, and used it to print *The Dime Catcher,* a Whig paper devoted to the promotion of the Presidential campaign of General Zachary Taylor. When the excitement of the campaign had passed, Ames, caught up by the furor aroused by the California gold strike, headed West with this press, via the Panama Canal. He stopped in Panama City briefly. Because of unfavorable reaction to his pub-

lishing efforts there, he soon resumed his journey to San Francisco. Later, he moved the press to San Diego and then to San Bernardino where, in 1861, he sold it to Major Edwin A. Sherman, the publisher of the *Patriot,* a Union-oriented paper. In response to the hostile political outlook of local residents, Sherman was soon forced to discontinue publication. He transported the press to Aurora, Nevada, and founded the *Esmeralda Star, circa* 1862. Here again he was faced with an unfavorable political atmosphere.

It was during this period that Mark Twain used the press. Later, it was sold and moved to Independence, California, where, after many more years of service, it was finally discarded in favor of more modern equipment.

This unique collection of American Colonial and Continental currency is by far the largest and most complete of its kind in existence. It was formed by Mr. James Cohen in the 19th century and contains, in fifteen volumes, almost every denomination of American paper money printed between 1709 and 1780.

At the age of 33, Henry Ford built his first automobile, which he called a "quadricycle," left. In the painting by Irving Bacon, below, he is shown in his back yard at 58 Bagley Avenue, Detroit. The car was belt-driven by a two-cylinder, three-horsepower, rear engine; Mr. Ford test drove it very early on the morning of June 4, 1896. This successful experiment gave him the confidence he needed to continue his automotive work and, ultimately, to found the Ford Motor Company. At the height of his career, in 1929, he founded The Edison Institute for the preservation of American history. Understandably, he devoted a large area of his museum to transportation history exemplified by the vast collection of boats, carriages, bicycles, locomotives, street cars, airplanes and automobiles, see opposite page. Many of these have great artistic, technical, or historic significance. Several of the airplanes pioneered in arctic and world explorations. Over three hundred steam, electric, and gasoline cars range from the earliest by Roper, Benz, Selden, and Duryea through the well-known marques of today.

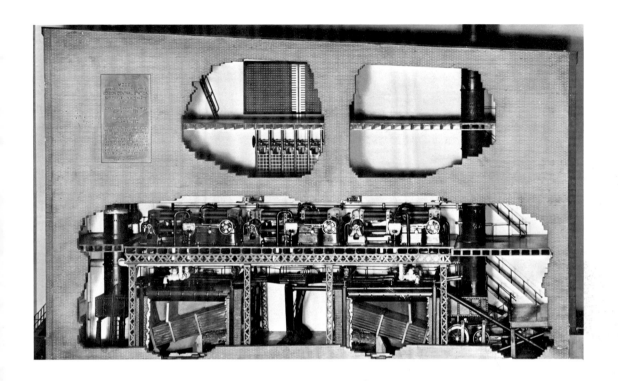

The photograph on the left was taken at the site of the original Pearl Street Central Station during the plaque dedication ceremony in 1917. On that occasion, the New York Edison Company decreed: "In a building on this site an electric plant supplying the first Edison underground central station system in this county, and forming the origin of New York's present electrical system, began operation on September 4, 1882, according to plans conceived and executed by Thomas Alva Edison." Left to right—William Meadowcroft, Wilson S. Howell, Thomas A. Edison, unidentified, Thomas C. Martin, Samuel G. Rhodes, and Richard Darlington. Above is a model of the world's first commercial central power station erected by Thomas A. Edison in 1881-1882 at 255 and 257 Pearl Street, New York City. Here commercial electrical service began on September 4, 1882,

at 3:00 p.m., supplying current for four hundred lamps in the waterfront area. At this station, Edison and his associates placed into commercial use, for the first time, a complete system of electrical engineering — its generation, control, distribution, measurement, and domestic consumption—necessitating the employment of efficient dynamos, regulators, feeders and main system, underground distribution, safety fuses, cutouts, switches, sockets, meters, motors and the incandescent lamp, all of which had been developed at the Menlo Park Laboratory between 1878 and 1882. Electricity on the 110-volt standard was supplied by six Edison "Jumbo" dynamos and fed to the customer by underground wiring.

The Pearl Street Station is thus the progenitor of all central stations which have been established in the world.

The fact that Henry Ford named his museum *The Edison Institute* indicates the importance he placed on the great inventor's contributions. This is emphasized by the preservation in Greenfield Village of the entire Edison Laboratory Compound from Menlo Park, New Jersey. It was in this laboratory on October 21, 1929, that Mr. Edison, accompanied by President Hoover and Mr. Ford, re-enacted the successful creation of the incandescent light. In addition to the scientific complex, the Menlo Park group includes Sarah Jordan's Boarding House. This house was wired for electricity by his workmen, and was the first residence in the world to have been lighted by incandescent electric lamps.

Although the chief emphasis of the collection is placed on the lighting and lamps used in the United States, a thorough history of lighting is shown, including choice lamps from China, Japan, India and Persia and primitive devices from Ancient Rome, Alaska and Hawaii.

Of the thousands of examples now in the collection, many are used in Greenfield Village and the Henry Ford Museum as they would have been originally. One large area installed in this manner is *The Light We Live By* exhibit. Here, in room-settings appropriate to the lighting devices, and in related displays, are illustrated the developments of illumination in America.

In the lighting display is shown a study collection of hundreds of objects, from ornate glass, brass, or tin chandeliers to pottery grease lamps, illustrated left, hurricane shades and pewter lamps. The superb Bennington pottery lamp illustrated, and the marked New England Glass Company lamp, are outsanding representatives of this major collection.

63

The bracket clock, shown left, is marked "Andrew Billings, Poughkeepsie, N.Y., 1795." The mahogany case, labeled by the firm of Slover and Kortright, New York, N.Y., is beautifully decorated with painting and satinwood inlays. It has elegant brass mounts. The clock's eight-day, spring-driven, one-hour-strike movement records, in addition to the time, the day, the date, the time of high and low tides and the lunar date.

Besides its obvious beauty, the piece has an historic association, being made for Cadwallader Colden who was Mayor of New York, 1818-1820, and later elected to the New York State Senate and the United States Congress.

Other Treasures not Illustrated

All non-illustrated entries in each category are listed approximately as they appear in the Museum's exhibit plan.

AMERICAN GOLD JEWELRY — Including the largest collection of mourning rings and pins

BRASS MUSICAL INSTRUMENTS — This collection, gathered by Daniel Sargent Pillsbury, Mount Vernon, New York, is the most comprehensive of its type known

CLOCKS AND WATCHES — A collection of over 3,500 examples which demonstrate the history of time-keeping

WOODWORKING HAND TOOLS — Used from the 17th century through the 19th century

LIGHTING COLLECTION — The largest comprehensive reference and research collection in existence, comprised of the world's largest collection of marked American betty lamps, of American pottery grease lamps, of canting lamps, of American patent lamps which includes a representative group of original patent office models and tags, of early candle and whale oil lanterns, of glass and crystal chandeliers and candelabra, and of free-blown and engraved hurricane shades

INCANDESCENT ELECTRIC LAMPS — The largest group known, including the William J. Hammer collection which was established by the Edison Pioneers, a group of Edison associates in his employ prior to 1885

TRANSPORTATION — The most comprehensive collection of material relating to the history of transportation

FORD ARCHIVES — The largest collection of records known related to a single individual, his family, his broad personal interests, his philanthropy and the world-wide business he founded

Decorated Press Cupboard, made for Hannah
Barnard, *circa* 1690, Connecticut Valley.

Unique Examples

All collection subject areas in Greenfield Village and the Henry Ford Museum contain unique materials. The library, for example, contains a typewritten letter on stationery "From the Laboratory of Thomas A. Edison, Orange, N. J.," dated December 29, 1920, and signed by Thomas A. Edison, in which he stated his belief in the importance of children being taught music in the home and in public schools.

The transportation collection contains Queen Victoria's gift to General Tom Thumb. It is a miniature brougham, made in 1875, and just large enough to accommodate the tiny gentleman and his lady.

In Greenfield Village is the Hanks Silk Mill, built in Mansfield, Connecticut, in 1810. This small structure was the first power mill to produce spun silk thread in America. Here, thin strands of silk were wound from the cocoons onto wooden reels before being twisted together into a single thread.

The question may be raised: what considerations or qualities make an object or a building unique? It cannot be merely that it represents a one-of-a-kind thing. Too many such articles exist which are poorly designed, odd-for-odds-sake, or which represent aberrant thought or craft techniques. A collectible unique example must demonstrate, above all, the craftsmanship of quality. It must be an object that illustrates accepted standards of function, design, purpose, and workmanship.

An object such as the Sarah Furman Warner quilted bedcover could properly be considered a Unique Example, a Masterpiece of Craftsmanship, or even an Historical Association piece. The 1690 Connecticut press cupboard can be equally looked upon as a Unique Example or a Masterpiece of Craftsmanship. However, for a museum collection the Unique Example must have the attributes of the Masterpiece.

Of particular note in this area are the Edward Sands Frost hooked rug stencil patterns, acquired by the Henry Ford Museum in 1958. Between 1868 and 1876, Frost, a Yankee tin peddler living in Biddeford, Maine, cut some 750 metal stencils to print more than 180 standard rug designs. Of these historic designs, 145 survive today. A creative interest of 19th Century America is thus continued, unbroken and unchanged, to the 20th Century.

Uniqueness can extend to every area of collecting. The Henry Ford Museum holds the Sandwich, Massachusetts, Glass Factory work records for the years 1825-1888; the Jenkins' rotating prism lens, an experimental television camera of 1923; the 1877 Selden Road Engine Patent, and the car, built *circa* 1905-1907, to prove the validity of the basic Selden automotive patent. Among the curiosa are a ten-man bicycle; a 1916 Woods Dual Power Car which combined the gasoline engine with an electric motor and electric batteries; *The Book of Martyrs*, hand produced by the Brothers of the Ephrata Cloisters, Pennsylvania, in 1748 and 1749. This first edition is the largest book printed in Colonial America.

The earliest known form of steam operated reciprocating engine, and the forerunner of every type of engine using a piston and connecting rod assembly, was invented by Thomas Newcomen, an ironmonger of Dartmouth, England. Newcomen commenced his experiments about 1705, and placed his first successful working engine at a local colliery in 1712. Having its origins in the pre-industrial era, this device was not utilized at first in a factory or mill setting. It was, instead, used as a means of pumping water from mine shafts, thus answering a great need which confronted domestic industry of this period.

The engine consists of a large *rocking beam* mounted upon suitable trunnions. One end of this beam is connected to a simple lift pump, and the other end to a piston moving in a vertical, open-topped cylinder. The pump end of the beam is weighted, causing the pis-

ton to rest at the top of the cylinder. When not in use, steam at a pressure from ½ to 21 pounds per square inch is admitted into the cylinder, heating its cylindrical wall. The steam is then stopped, and simultaneously a jet of cold water is sprayed into this chamber, causing a partial vacuum, beneath the piston, resulting from interior condensation. The atmosphere, being of greater pressure above, forces the piston down in the cylinder, causing the pump to rise on the other end, thus accomplishing the working stroke.

Oliver Evans, one of the most noted steam engineers in the early days of the republic, issued the license, shown above, on November 10, 1812, to the "Mariatta Steam Mill Company," at Mariatta, Ohio. This interesting document covered the terms of sale and subsequent operation of a twenty horsepower reciprocating, walking beam engine.

The Boston and Sandwich Glass Company, Sandwich, Massachusetts (1825-1888), was probably the most famous glass house in the United States. Vast quantities of wares were shipped all over the world. Articles of Incorporation, ledgers and account books in the Museum define much of the company's business. This cream pitcher, *circa* 1830, is the only known example of opalescent three-mold glass.

This high-backed, mahogany, Chippendale open armchair was made in Philadelphia by Thomas Affleck, about 1765. It served as the Speaker's Chair at the Supreme Court Chamber in the State House (today called Independence Hall). The rococo shaping of the back is like that on chairs made by Affleck for Governor John Penn. The rope molding and bead-and-reel carving on the legs and arm supports is like other Supreme Court chairs. This piece is believed to be unique in the combination of the shaped back with the above-mentioned carved motifs. The chair was purchased by Dr. Thomas Chalkley James (1766-1835) after 1812, when the State House furnishings were moved from Philadelphia to Harrisburg, the capitol of Pennsylvania. It then passed into the collections of Mr. and Mrs. Charles B. Lewis and of Reginald M. Lewis, prior to its purchase by the Henry Ford Museum. The chair is illustrated in Hornor's *Blue Book of Philadelphia Furniture.*

Edward Sands Frost epitomizes the modern day idea of New England ingenuity. Noting the housewife's need for patterns on which she could construct hooked rugs, he devised a series of metal stencils from which one hundred eighty-two designs could be formed. The patterns range from common fruit and linear motifs to various animal forms and more complicated geometric designs. A single stencil would be used for the central pattern, with parts of others chosen for the border and other minor motifs. Each one would be placed on the burlap background and transferred to it separately. Frost lived in Biddeford, Maine, and after the Civil War, sold his patterns in the general area. The brochure, shown right, was part of his advertising material and illustrates many of his designs such as the one shown right. The patterns are again being printed on burlap at the Cotton Gin Mill in Greenfield Village and are available to the public.

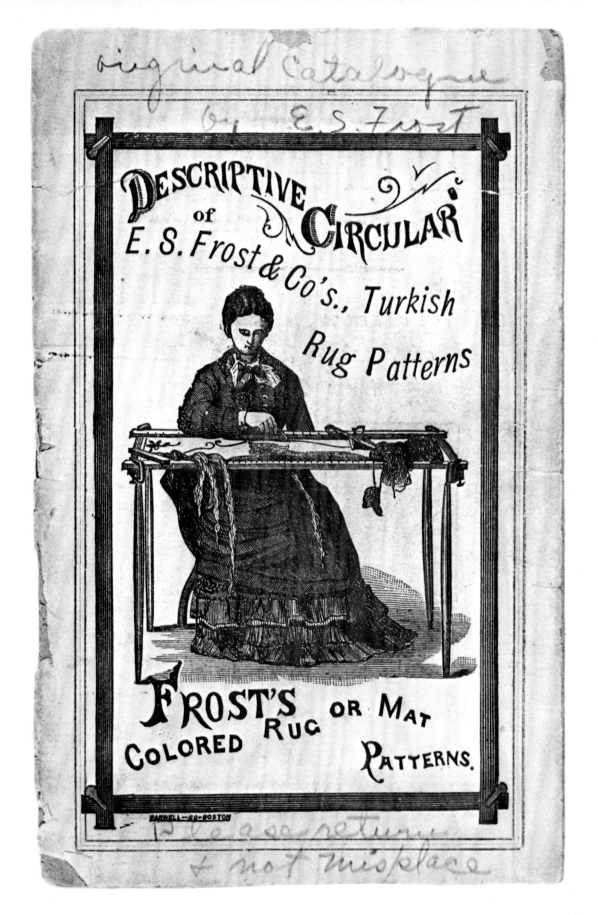

DESCRIPTIVE CIRCULAR of E. S. Frost & Co's., Turkish Rug Patterns

FROST'S COLORED RUG OR MAT PATTERNS.

BARNELL—SQ—BOSTON

Although experiments with "television" were made as early as 1883 by Nipkow, the phenomenon of transmitting pictures by wireless did not become a reality until the invention of the rotating, prismatic scanning disc set by the Washington scientist, Francis Jenkins, in 1923. On Sunday, June 14, 1923, the *Washington Sunday Star* reported: "'Radio Vision' long the fantastic dream of science became an accomplished feat yesterday afternoon with Secretary of the Navy Wilbur and other high government officials witnessing the feat. With the aid of a remarkable apparatus invented by . . . Francis Jenkins the Secretary of the Navy, Dr. George M. Burgess, Director of the Bureau of Standards; Admiral D. W. Taylor, Captain Paul Foley of the National Research Laboratory and others actually saw by radio an object set in motion several miles distant in front of a 'radio eye' . . . ."

This original apparatus was donated to The Edison Institute in 1940 by Mrs. Francis Jenkins.

Sarah Furman Warner of Greenfield Hill, Connecticut, created this outstanding piece of needlework probably during the last years of the 18th century. There is no record of the time consumed by her efforts, but the precise and intricate design, her superb choice of fabrics for the applique, and her meticulous stitches created a folk art masterpiece.

Other Treasures not Illustrated

All non-illustrated entries in each category are listed approximately as they appear in the Museum's exhibit plan.

DOUBLE BUTTERFLY TABLE — The only known example having two butterfly supports on each side, *circa* 1750

TILE-TOP MIXING TABLE — The larger of two known Queen Anne mixing tables with Biblical Delft tiles

FIRE SCREEN TABLE — An adjustable wallpaper fire screen on a Chippendale end table is an extreme rarity

JACOB EBY CLOCK — The bow front on this Hepplewhite tall case clock is unique

"THE BUSY WORLD" — An animated display of 365 hand-carved wooden figures complete with original wagon and advertising banner made by David Hoy of Walton, New York, *circa* 1835

BLUE STAFFORDSHIRE PLATTER — Made by James and Ralph Clews, Cobridge, England, *circa* 1830; it is 20½ inches wide and decorated with a transfer-printed view of Detroit enclosed within a unique double border

BRASS GOLDSMITH'S SCALES — Made by Philip Syng, Jr., Philadelphia, Pennsylvania, *circa* 1750

SILVER CORNET — Made by J. Lathrop Allen in 1845 for Harvey Dodsworth; the only example known to have been produced with a five-valve rotary action

1932 THREE-CENT WASHINGTON COIL STAMPS — A comprehensive collection of plate varieties found in this issue

MINIATURE FARM MACHINERY: THRESHING MACHINE AND OTHER EQUIPMENT — Made by Henry Ford for his grandchildren

HEDGEHOG THRESHER — One of the earliest mechanized threshing devices

BAR OF PIG IRON — Marked "Elizabeth Furnace" by Henry William Stiegel at his 18th Century works, Lancaster County, Pennsylvania

SET OF TEMPLATES — Used by Dolphus Drake, Bedford Co., Penn., *circa* 1825, for inlay work on Kentucky rifles

WROUGHT IRON DIES — Found in Southeastern Ohio, they are the only known set used to produce wrought iron Betty lamps

SHEET COPPER BETTY LAMP — Unique prototype made by Peter Derr, *circa* 1828-31, at Bernville, Penn.

BRASS ARGAND LAMP AND TRIVET BY H. N. HOOPER & CO. — Adapted for use as a bunsen burner by R. Finelly in his apothecary shop at Boston, Massachusetts, *circa* 1800

MINIATURE BROUGHAM — Presented in 1875 by Queen Victoria to General Tom Thumb

1877 SELDEN ROAD ENGINE PATENT AND CAR — Automobile built, *circa* 1907, to prove the validity of the basic patent

1896 "ORITEN" BICYCLE — The only bicycle in the world built for ten riders

1910 AMERICAN TRUCK — Constructed with 4-wheel chain-drive and 4-wheel steering capability

1914 FORD CYCLECAR — Miniature Model T which proved Henry Ford's ability to produce a cyclecar, thereby discouraging further competition

1916 WOODS DUAL POWER CAR — Combined gasoline engine, electric motor and electric batteries as motive power

THE TWELVE ORIGINAL STOCK CERTIFICATES OF FORD MOTOR COMPANY — Issued June 26, 1903, and accompanied by contemporary photographs of the original owners

BLACK BOX — In this device, Edison demonstrated his 1875 discovery of Etheric Force, which is the basis of modern wireless transmission

HAND-OPERATED VACUUM PUMP — Used by Thomas Edison in 1879 for exhausting his early Bell jars containing platinum lamp filaments

1891 BOOK OF INSTRUCTIONS — *Description of Methods Used in Making Standard Lamps* by John W. Howell, giving procedures for making a bamboo lamp

Contributing Staff
for this Publication

Dr. Donald A. Shelley, *President*

Robert G. Wheeler, *Vice-President*
Research and Interpretation

George O. Bird
Curator, Ceramics and Glass

Robert Bishop
Curator, Furniture

Carleton W. Brown
Consulting Curator, Lighting and Tools

William Distin
Curator, Special Collections and Registrar

Katharine Bryant Hagler
Research Assistant, Furniture

Leslie Henry
Curator, Transportation

Robert Koolakian
Assistant Curator, Communications

Walter E. Simmons, II
Assistant Curator, Metals

Jerome I. Smith
Librarian

Designed and Edited by Robert Bishop
Editorial Assistant—Patricia Coblentz
Photography by Charles Miller, Carl Malotka, Rudolph Ruzicska
Typography by Stephen Typesetting, Detroit, Michigan
Printed by Litho-Art, Inc., Madison Heights, Michigan